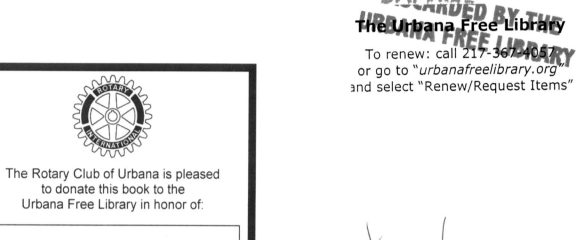

The Rotary Club of Urbana is pleased
to donate this book to the
Urbana Free Library in honor of:

Thank You
Rotary Club!

## U.S. SYMBOLS

# THE PLEDGE OF ALLEGIANCE

by Tyler Monroe

**Consulting Editor:** Gail Saunders-Smith, PhD

CAPSTONE PRESS
a capstone imprint

Pebble Plus is published by Capstone Press,
1710 Roe Crest Drive, North Mankato, Minnesota 56003
www.capstonepub.com

**Library of Congress Cataloging-in-Publication Data**
Monroe, Tyler, 1976–
    The pledge of allegiance / by Tyler Monroe.
        pages cm.—(Pebble plus. U.S. symbols)
    Includes bibliographical references and index.
    Summary: "Simple text and full-color photographs briefly describe The Pledge of Allegiance and its role as a national symbol"--Provided by publisher.
    ISBN 978-1-4765-3090-1 (library binding)—ISBN 978-1-4765-3539-5 (pbk.)—ISBN 978-1-4765-3512-8 (ebook pdf)
    1.  Bellamy, Francis. Pledge of Allegiance to the Flag—Juvenile literature. 2.  Flags—United States—Juvenile literature.  I. Title.
    JC346.M66 2014
    323.6'5—dc23                                                                                                   2013001823

**Editorial Credits**
Erika L. Shores, editor; Lori Bye, designer; Svetlana Zhurkin, media researcher; Eric Manske, production specialist

**Photo Credits**
Capstone Studio: Karon Dubke, cover; Corbis: Bettmann, 17; Getty Images: SuperStock, 19; iStockphotos: Jacom Stephens, 1, sjlocke, 5, 15; Library of Congress, 8, 13; Newscom: Everett Collection, 11; Shutterstock: Spirit of America, 21, Suat Gursozlu (stars), cover and throughout; Watertown Free Public Library, 9

## Note to Parents and Teachers

The U.S. Symbols set supports national social studies standards related to people, places, and culture. This book describes and illustrates the Pledge of Allegiance. The images support early readers in understanding the text. The repetition of words and phrases helps early readers learn new words. This book also introduces early readers to subject-specific vocabulary words, which are defined in the Glossary section. Early readers may need assistance to read some words and to use the Table of Contents, Glossary, Read More, Internet Sites, and Index sections of the book.

Printed in China by Nordica.
0413/CA21300494
032013      007226NORDF13

# TABLE OF CONTENTS

# A Promise to America

The Pledge of Allegiance is
a promise. People say
the pledge to show loyalty
and respect to the United States.

The pledge's words show a person's pride in being a U.S. citizen. But saying the pledge isn't a law. Americans don't have to say the Pledge of Allegiance.

I pledge Allegiance to the flag
of the United States of America
and to the Republic for which it stands,
one nation under God, indivisible,
with liberty and justice for all.

# Who Wrote the Pledge?

In 1892 Francis Bellamy wrote the Pledge of Allegiance. He wanted students to say it on Columbus Day. He mailed copies of the pledge to schools around the country.

Francis Bellamy

A Columbus Day parade in 1892 celebrated Christopher Columbus reaching the Americas 400 years earlier.

Students and teachers liked the pledge. Children started saying it every day. It became a tradition in U.S. schools.

# The Flag Code

Congress included the pledge
in the U.S. Flag Code in 1942.
The code is a list of rules for
using the American flag correctly.

The code says most people
should take off their hats
when they say the pledge.
Only people in the military keep
their hats on during the pledge.

Military members salute
the flag during the pledge.

Changes have been made
to the pledge over the years.
In 1923 the words "my flag"
were changed to "the flag of
the United States of America."

The pledge in 1923

The PLEDGE to the FLAG

I PLEDGE ALLEGIANCE
to the FLAG of the
UNITED STATES of AMERICA
and to the REPUBLIC for which
IT STANDS
ONE NATION INDIVISIBLE
with LIBERTY and JUSTICE
for ALL

# The Symbol Today

President Dwight D. Eisenhower
asked Congress to change
the pledge again in 1954.
The words "under God" were
added after the word "nation."

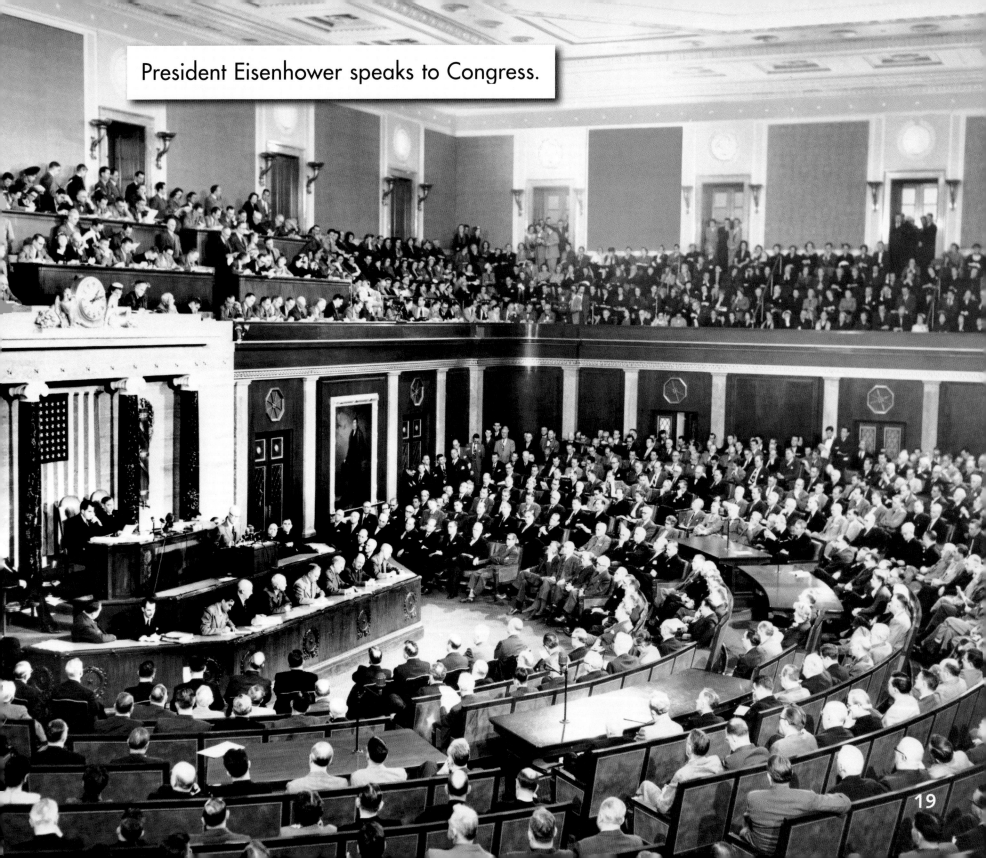

President Eisenhower speaks to Congress.

People can say the pledge anytime. People stand and face the American flag. They hold their right hands over their hearts as they say the words.

21

# Glossary

**allegiance**—loyal support for something

**citizen**—a member of a country or state who has the right to live there

**Congress**—the part of the U.S. government that makes laws

**loyalty**—support for someone or something

**military**—the armed forces of a state or country

**pledge**—to make a promise

**pride**—a feeling of happiness about someone or something

**respect**—a feeling that shows you value someone or something

**salute**—to give a sign of respect

**tradition**—a custom, idea, or belief passed down through time

# Read More

**Harris, Nancy.** *The Pledge of Allegiance.* Patriotic Symbols. Chicago: Heinemann Library, 2008.

**Pearl, Norman.** *The Pledge of Allegiance.* American Symbols. Minneapolis: Picture Window Books, 2007.

**Tourville, Amanda Doering.** *The Pledge of Allegiance.* Edina, Minn.: Magic Wagon, 2008.

# Internet Sites

FactHound offers a safe, fun way to find Internet sites related to this book. All of the sites on FactHound have been researched by our staff.

Here's all you do:

Visit *www.facthound.com*

Type in this code: 9781476530901

Super-cool stuff! Check out projects, games and lots more at **www.capstonekids.com**

# Critical Thinking Using the Common Core

1. Why did Francis Bellamy want students to say the Pledge of Allegiance on Columbus Day? (Key Ideas and Details)

2. Why is it good to have rules for using the American flag correctly? (Key Ideas and Details)

3. In addition to the flag, to what else might you pledge? (Integration of Knowledge and Ideas)

## Index

Word Count: 223
Grade: 1
Early-Intervention Level: 22